CORPORATE AMERICA

TESLA

Tammy Gagne

LIGHTBOX
openlightbox.com

LIGHTBOX

Go to
www.openlightbox.com
and enter this book's
unique code.

ACCESS CODE

LBW36935

Lightbox is an all-inclusive digital solution for the teaching and learning of curriculum topics in an original, groundbreaking way. Lightbox is based on National Curriculum Standards.

STANDARD FEATURES OF LIGHTBOX

AUDIO High-quality narration using text-to-speech system

ACTIVITIES Printable PDFs that can be emailed and graded

SLIDESHOWS Pictorial overviews of key concepts

VIDEOS Embedded high-definition video clips

WEBLINKS Curated links to external, child-safe resources

TRANSPARENCIES Step-by-step layering of maps, diagrams, charts, and timelines

INTERACTIVE MAPS Interactive maps and aerial satellite imagery

QUIZZES Ten multiple choice questions that are automatically graded and emailed for teacher assessment

KEY WORDS Matching key concepts to their definitions

Contents

Introduction

Tesla is the world's leading producer of fully electric automobiles. In 2017, the company became the top-selling automaker in the United States. It ranks fourth globally. Tesla designs, manufactures, and markets its vehicles to customers in North America, Europe, and Asia. Tesla's cars have attracted attention for being an **environmentally friendly** vehicle option. Unlike gas-powered vehicles, electric vehicles do not produce carbon emissions. This helps reduce the amount of pollution in the air.

Tesla makes several models of electric vehicles. These include the Model S family sedan, the Model X sport utility vehicle, and the Model 3, which is Tesla's version of an economy car. In addition to being energy-efficient, Tesla vehicles are known for their **high-end** performance and cutting-edge technology.

Tesla is named for scientist **Nikola Tesla**, who is best known for his ***work with electricity***.

In 2016, Tesla sold about ***76,000 cars worldwide***.

Tesla has more than ***280 stores and galleries*** **around the world**.

In 2013, the ***Model S*** became the first electric car to ever win ***Motor Trend*** **magazine's** ***Car of the Year award***.

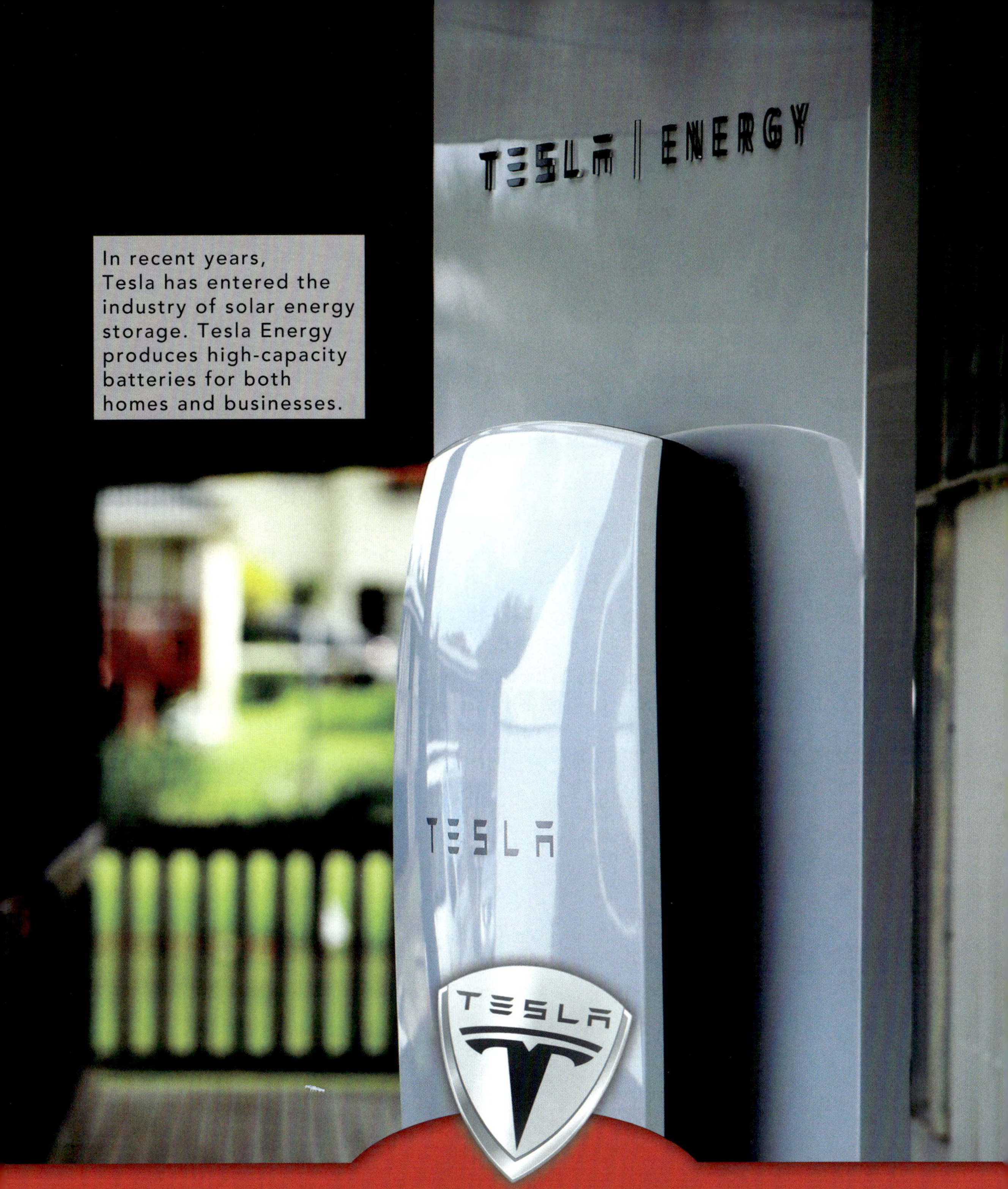

In recent years, Tesla has entered the industry of solar energy storage. Tesla Energy produces high-capacity batteries for both homes and businesses.

Founding Date	Became Public	Opening Price	Stock Symbol
2003	June 29, 2010	$17.00 USD	nasdaq: TSLA

Beginnings

When most people think of Tesla, they also think of the company's leader, Elon Musk. Musk, however, is not the founder of the company. **Entrepreneurs** Martin Eberhard and Marc Tarpenning started Tesla in July 2003. They wanted to create a high-performance car that did not depend on **fossil fuels**. The two men founded the company and ran it together until April 2004. This was when Musk **invested** $6.5 million in the business and became its **chairman of the board**.

Musk was confident that Tesla had something valuable to offer the car-buying public. About a year after his first investment, he put another $9 million into the growing company. At this time, the company was developing its plans for the Tesla Roadster, a high-end sports car. This battery-powered automobile could be driven 250 miles (402 kilometers) on a single charge. Tesla began selling the Roadster to the public in 2008. Priced at $100,000, it was too expensive for many people interested in buying an environmentally friendly vehicle. Still, Tesla's first electric vehicle brought a great deal of attention to this new car company.

Elon Musk became Tesla's chief executive officer (CEO) in 2008, the same year the Roadster was launched.

In 2010, Musk decided to take the company public. This means selling stock in a company to raise **capital**, particularly for new projects. The Tesla Model S was one such project. This battery-powered car differed from the Roadster in a few key areas. Instead of a sports car, the Model S was a sedan, intended for family use. It was also less than half the price of the Roadster. With this new direction and new price point, Tesla was ready to bring electric cars to the masses.

"I couldn't bring myself to buy a car that got 18 miles [29 km] to the gallon [4 liters] at a time when wars in the Middle East seemed to somehow involve oil and the arguments for global warming were becoming undeniable."

– Martin Eberhard,
Tesla Co-founder

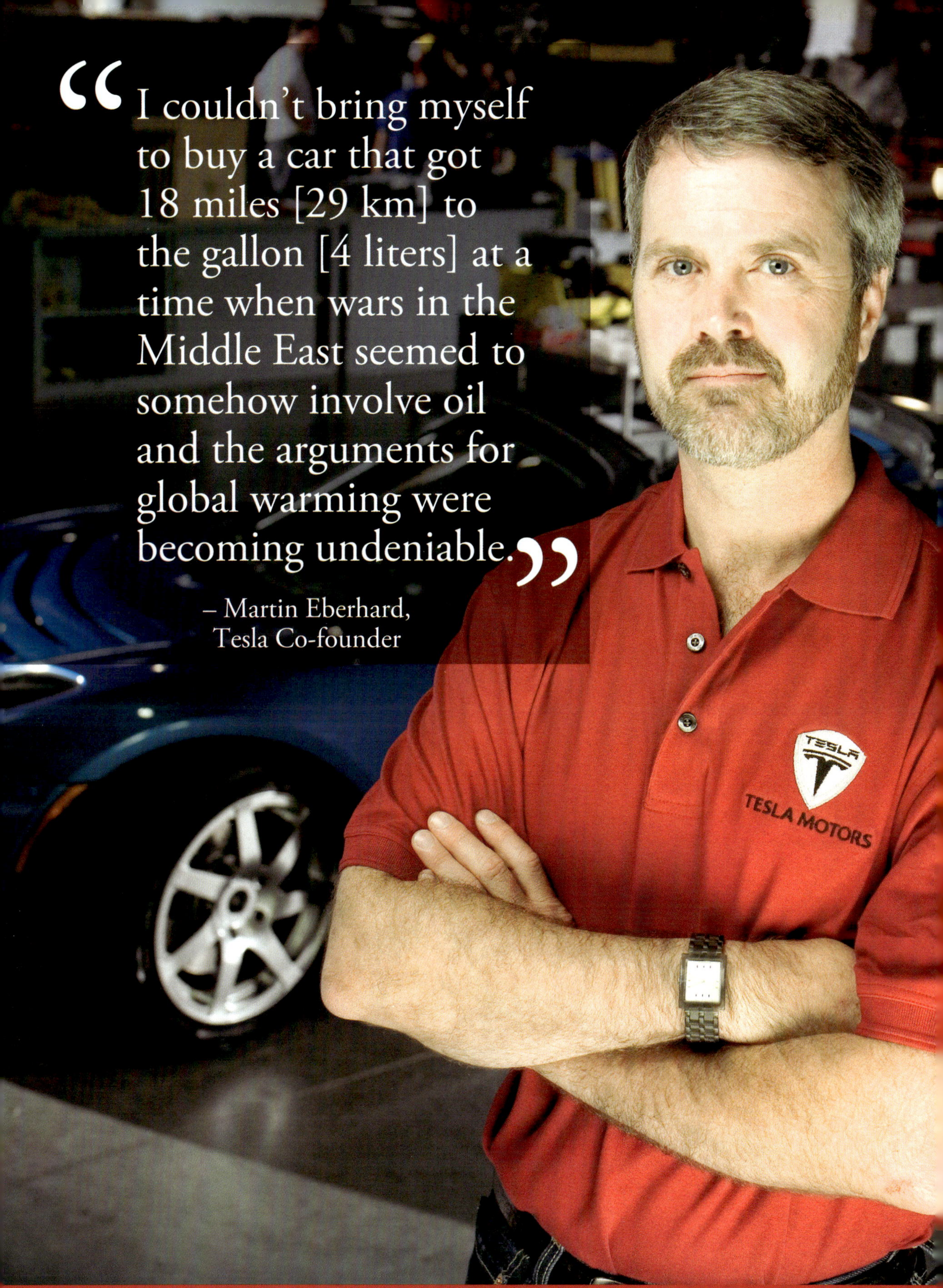

Corporate Timeline

Tesla has come a long way since the company's creation. The U.S. automobile manufacturer is one of the most talked-about companies in the world today. Tesla has taken advantage of this momentum by **diversifying** its business interests into the realm of energy storage. The company continues to seek new directions and new ways to extend its influence.

2003

Open for Business
Martin Eberhard and Marc Tarpenning found Tesla.

2004

Adding a Chair
Elon Musk becomes chairman of the board for Tesla.

2006

An Advanced Model
Tesla introduces its Roadster model.

2008

Leading the Way
Elon Musk moves into the CEO position.

2009

Energy Assistance
Tesla borrows $465 million from the United States Department of Energy to produce all-electric vehicles and to develop a facility that will manufacture parts for the vehicles.

2010

Going Public
Tesla becomes the first U.S. car company to offer its stock to the public since Ford Motor Company in 1956.

2012

A Tesla First
Tesla introduces the Model X SUV, its first all-wheel drive sport utility vehicle.

2013

Making Good
Tesla repays its government loan nine years ahead of schedule.

2016

A New Price Point
Tesla begins taking orders for its most affordable car to date, the Model 3. The car is priced at $35,000.

2017

Top of the Heap
Forbes magazine names Tesla's X 100D the vehicle of the year.

Tesla Today

Tesla continues to add to its list of accomplishments. In 2017, the Tesla Model X became the first sport utility vehicle to earn a five-star crash rating in every category and subcategory from the National Highway Traffic Safety Administration (NHTSA). The Model X's top rating means that, out of any SUV tested, it has the lowest likelihood of injury in the event of a crash. Customers who choose a Tesla can feel confident in knowing they will be driving a vehicle that is both kind to the environment and safe for its drivers and passengers. The only vehicle that has a lower risk of injury is Tesla's Model S.

Besides improving safety features, the company is also working hard to make electric cars convenient for people to use. One of the main concerns people have about owning an electric vehicle is the need to charge it. While owners of gas-powered vehicles can stop at the nearest gas station, drivers of battery-powered cars must plug their vehicles into a power source. This used to mean returning home before their vehicle's charge dipped too low. Now, however, Tesla has created public charging stations for its consumers. Called Superchargers, these stations allow drivers to travel farther without worrying about running out of power. A 30-minute visit to a Supercharger station can give a Tesla driver up to another 170 miles (274 km) of range.

At its core, Tesla remains a company committed to the environment. It continues to search for new ways to create a more **sustainable** world. Launched in 2017, Tesla's Solar Roof system enables a home to absorb energy from the Sun and use it to power the home's electrical devices. Solar Roof can be paired with a battery storage system developed by Tesla called Powerwall. The storage system makes it possible for homeowners to collect energy during the day and use it whenever they need it. This allows homeowners to save money on electricity bills and to use a renewable form of energy.

By the end of 2017, Tesla had opened 10,000 Supercharger stations around the world.

> "You want to be extra rigorous about making the best possible thing you can. Find everything that's wrong with it and fix it. Seek negative feedback, particularly from friends."
>
> – Elon Musk,
> Tesla Chief Executive
> Officer (CEO)

A World of Tesla

Tesla vehicles are sold around the world. However, the company's operations currently remain mainly in the United States. In recent years, the company has started taking steps to set up foreign offices and manufacturing facilities.

1 **Corporate Headquarters** Located in Palo Alto, California, Tesla's head office is 1 million square feet (92,902 square meters) in area. The building originally belonged to computer company Hewlett Packard.

2 **Tesla Factory** Tesla produces its vehicles at its factory in Fremont, California. Most vehicle parts are also made at this location. The facility currently covers 5.3 million square feet (492,386 sq. m).

3 **Gigafactory 1** Tesla is currently building a **gigafactory** outside Reno, Nevada. When completed, the factory will manufacture the **lithium-ion batteries** required to run Tesla vehicles.

4 **European Headquarters** Tesla's European headquarters is located in Amsterdam, Netherlands. The office is located about 70 miles (113 km) away from the company's European distribution center in Tilburg.

5 **Asian Factory** In 2017, Tesla announced that it was in discussions to establish its first Asian factory in Shanghai, China. China is currently the world's largest maker of electric vehicles and has the largest auto market in the world.

Branding Tesla

Tesla is no ordinary automaker. In addition to offering cutting-edge products, the company has created an image for itself that is unlike any other automaker. Consumers have come to link the Tesla name to innovative technology, luxury, and environmental sustainability. Each of these features is valuable on its own, but it is the combination of all three that gives the company its unique **brand** identity.

Electric Luxury Before Tesla was founded, the public saw the electric car as a down-to-earth vehicle choice. Tesla wanted people to see electric cars as exciting and sophisticated. Its designers began creating vehicles that would attract upscale buyers. Tesla cars are now known for their sleek design and high-end features. In creating a luxury electric car, Tesla has made saving the environment trendy. People who may not have bought an electric car in the past are now lining up to make the purchase.

Advanced Technology Tesla knows that, to stand out in a crowded market, it has to show potential buyers that it can offer perks that other automakers do not. The company works hard to develop technology that will pique interest in its products. For example, there are not many cars on the market that can be updated through a computer download. Tesla promotes itself as a forward-thinking company. It wants people to see the company and its products as innovative, unique, and dynamic.

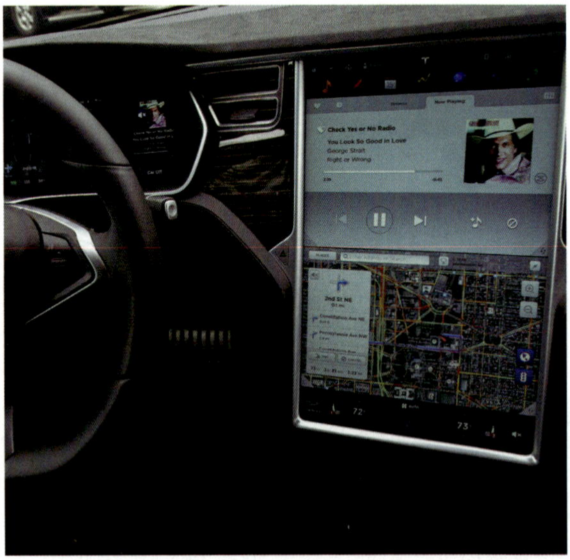

Staying Grounded Tesla remains a company focused on sustainability. It is continually working to convince people that **clean energy** is the way of the future. As sustainability is a key part of its brand, the company concentrates its efforts on developing products that promote this cause. While the company began by developing electric cars, it has now branched out into other areas that show its concern for the environment, including solar panels and power storage units.

TESLA

Company Name

Nikola Tesla is best known for contributing to the design of the **alternating current** system. This electrical system is integral to the operation of Tesla vehicles. The company has stated that, without the scientist, Tesla vehicles likely would not exist.

Company Logo

At first glance, the Tesla **logo** looks like the letter "T." Most people understand the "T" to stand for the company's name. However, the logo is actually designed to represent the cross-section of an electric motor.

Company Slogan

Companies often use **slogans** to sell their products and their brands. Tesla is different, however. Instead of a catchy phrase, the company markets its cars by highlighting three key features the cars possess. The phrasing is simple and to the point, "Quickest acceleration. Longest range. The safest cars ever."

The Art of Selling

Tesla has taken a unique approach to selling its products. While other companies spend millions of dollars on advertising, Tesla has let its many fans spread the word for the company instead. Millions of people follow, like, and post about the company on social media. Besides being effective, this strategy also allows the company to spend its money on product development instead of pricey ad campaigns.

The Direct Approach Tesla operates under a direct sales model. This means that the company deals directly with its customers and not through third parties. As it does not use dealerships, Tesla has set up showrooms for people to visit. Here, they can talk with Tesla employees face-to-face and ask questions of people who are experts on the company's vehicles. If a customer wants to take a car out for a test drive, he or she must go online to make the request. A customer who wants to buy a Tesla must also do so through the company's website.

Creating Community Tesla's website is full of information on the company's products. Potential customers can access details on every vehicle with ease. They can also use the site to interact with people who have already bought Tesla vehicles. Tesla encourages customers to post their comments, questions, and reviews to the site. In this way, the company is building its own sales community, allowing word of mouth to promote its vehicles. Potential customers are more likely to respect the opinions of people who have already purchased a Tesla over those of a traditional salesperson.

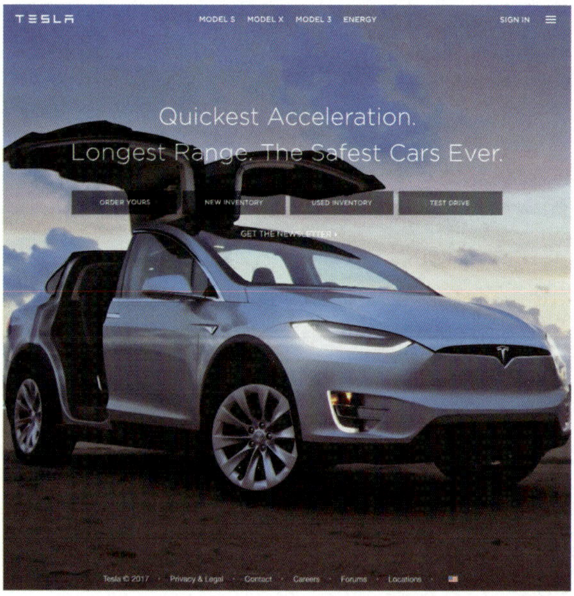

Musk Media Elon Musk is the face of Tesla. People get to know the company through him. Having a magnetic personality at the helm of Tesla gives the company a strong marketing presence. From electric cars to commercial space flights, Musk has built his reputation on being an innovative and creative thinker. He also knows how to communicate his ideas in ways that attract attention and interest. His use of social media has brought much attention to Tesla and its products. Musk not only provides updates on new products, but also lets his followers know the latest happenings at the company.

Within weeks of announcing its Model 3, Tesla had almost **400,000 preorders** for the car.

In 2016, ***Tesla buyers*** had an average household income of **$271,000**.

Elon Musk has more than **13 million followers** on Twitter.

Competitors

The automobile industry has been highly competitive since the first cars were mass produced at the start of the 20th century. The industry is driven by technology. While Tesla is currently the leader in electric cars, several other automakers are also building their own electric or **hybrid** vehicles in an effort to compete.

STOCK SYMBOL nyse: GM

General Motors has been making automobiles for more than a century. This U.S. company owns several brands of automobiles, including Chevrolet. In 2016, Chevrolet released its own electric car, the Chevy Bolt EV. The Bolt can run for more than 200 miles (322 km) on a single charge. It has quickly become one of GM's most successful vehicles.

STOCK SYMBOL tyo: NSANY

Japanese automobile manufacturer Nissan has also introduced an electric model. Pricing for the Nissan Leaf starts at about $5,000 less than the Tesla Model 3. However, the Leaf can only be driven for about 150 miles (241 km) before it must be recharged. Nissan has announced that it will increase the range for its 2019 model.

STOCK SYMBOL etr: BMW

Founded in 1916, BMW is a German company that makes a variety of vehicles, ranging from cars to motorcycles. It is also the parent company for the luxury brand Rolls Royce. Besides competing with Tesla in the luxury vehicle category, BMW has also entered the electric car market. Its BMW i3 model debuted at the Frankfurt auto show in 2013, along with its i8 hybrid model.

Comparison Chart

Businesses keep records to track their **assets**, **liabilities**, **profits**, and losses. Companies use this data to guide expansion and cost-cutting decisions. Investors use the information to help them decide where to invest their money. They will also refer to a company's **market capitalization** to gauge public confidence in the business.

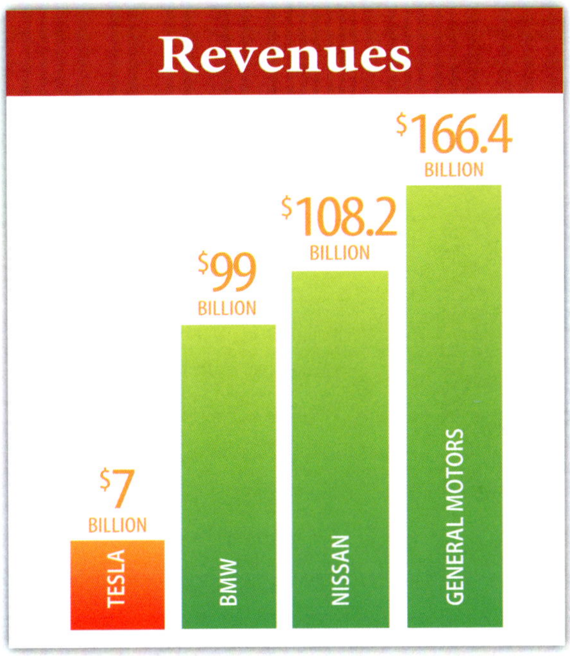

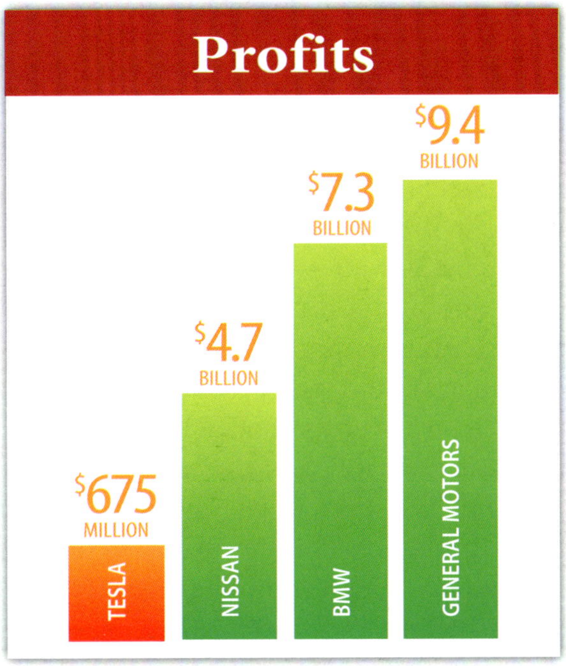

2016 Figures

Innovation and Technology

Electric Motors

While Tesla is not the first or only company to build cars with electric motors, it has been innovative with the technology involved. Like a laptop, Tesla's motors are powered by lithium-ion batteries. Cells within these batteries produce electricity. This electricity is sent to an electronics system, which controls the current and voltage. The electricity is then flowed toward electromagnets inside the motor, which work to turn the shaft that controls the movement of the wheels.

Speed

Tesla's electric vehicles have completely destroyed the longtime belief that battery-powered automobiles are slow. In fact, Tesla's Model S is the fastest car in production in the world today. It can go from 0 to 60 miles (0 to 97 km) per hour in just 2.28 seconds. That is faster than sports cars such as Ferrari's LaFerrari and the Porsche 918 Spyder, which each costs about $1 million. Tesla gives much of the credit for the Model S's speed to an upgraded version of its battery. This new battery can handle higher voltages without catching fire or melting.

Low Maintenance

In addition to being better for the environment, owning a Tesla is also easier on its owner. People who own gas-powered vehicles must perform a fair amount of regular maintenance on their automobiles. Oil needs to be changed about every 3,000 miles (4,828 km). Gas-powered vehicles also need new brake pads and other **disposable** items as they wear out. Tesla vehicles, however, require very little maintenance. In fact, only six parts on a Tesla need to be replaced regularly. These are its four tires and two windshield wiper blades.

Self-Driving Vehicles

The idea of a self-driving car once seemed like science fiction. Tesla has made it a reality, however, with its Autopilot feature. Autopilot addresses the issue of safety on the road, one of the main concerns people have about the vehicles. The technology within Autopilot works to sense the car's surroundings. If the sensors indicate that the vehicle is in danger of a collision, they send a message to the car's computing system to activate the brakes. In most cases, the computer can detect and avoid obstacles faster than a driver could in the same situation.

Giving Back

As a company that focuses on creating community, Tesla works to make the world a better place. Its charitable work ranges from traditional to innovative. The company is known to donate money to worthy causes, such as education. It has also given away company secrets in the name of **philanthropy**.

Sharing Ideas When companies develop new technology, they usually apply for a patent. This document confirms the details of the technology and registers it as the company's property. This gives the company the right to decide who can use the technology and under what conditions. In 2014, Tesla announced that it was releasing its patents to the public. It stated that keeping the technology to itself was not in line with its goal of encouraging sustainable transportation. The company now welcomes other companies to view the patents and use them to develop their own technology. In doing so, Tesla hopes that more people will see the advantages of electric vehicles.

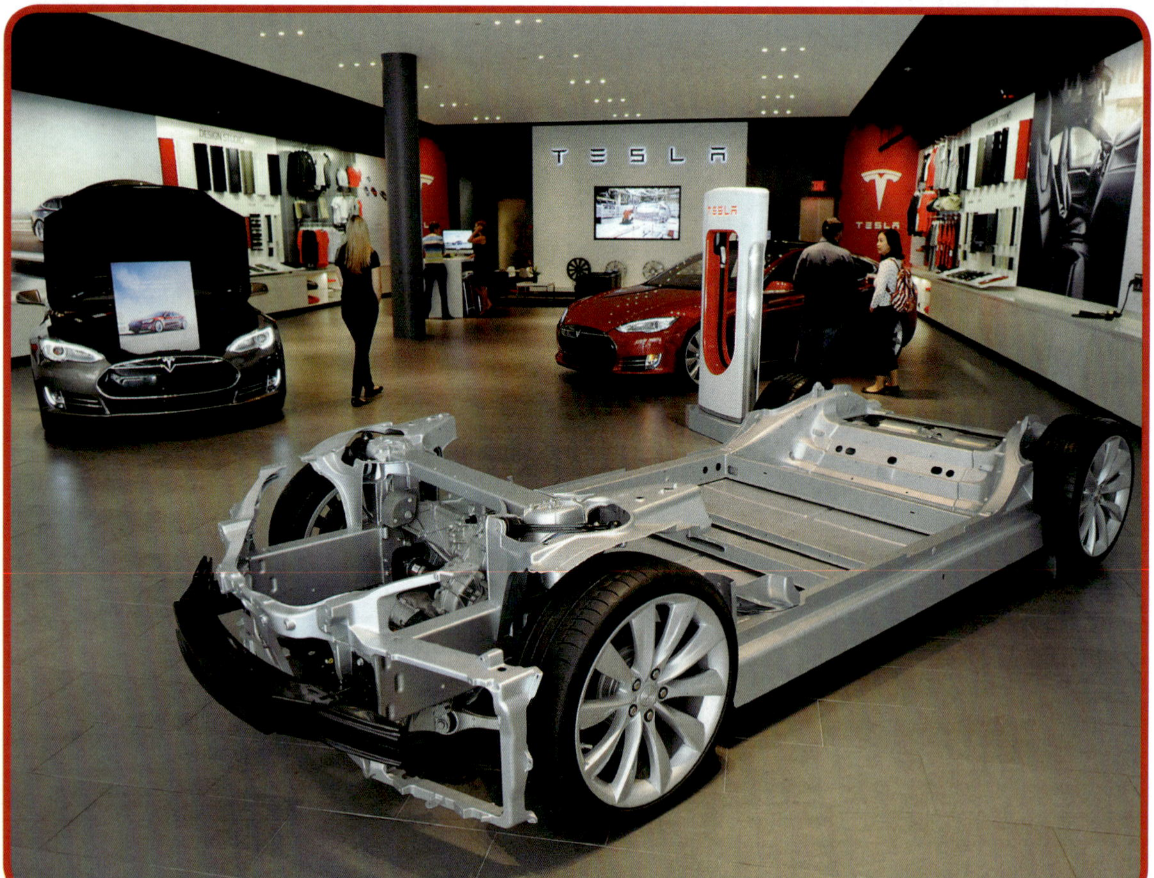

Looking to the Future Tesla has shown the importance it places on education through its many donations to schools and training programs. In 2014, for instance, the company signed an agreement with the Nevada state government to provide $37.5 million to the state's Department of Education over five years. The money will be invested in the STEM subjects of science, technology, engineering, and mathematics. More recently, Tesla signed an agreement with Farmingdale State College in 2017 to provide students in the college's automotive programs with **internships** at Tesla. There, they will gain first-hand knowledge of the technology inside Tesla's vehicles.

In 2014, Elon Musk donated **$1 million** toward the construction of a science museum in **Long Island, New York,** to honor the work of Nikola Tesla.

In 2014, Tesla gave **$1 million** to the University of Nevada Las Vegas for **battery research**.

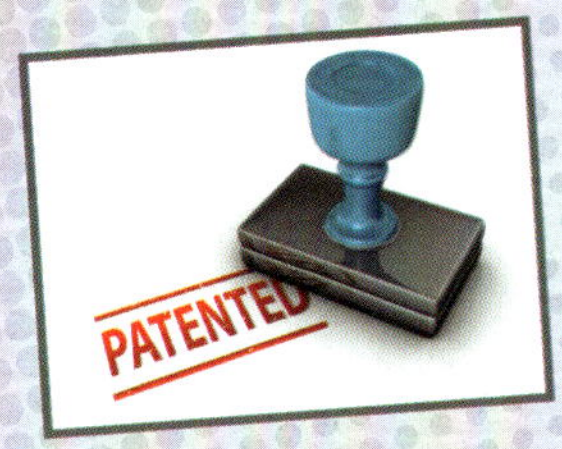

At the time of their release, Tesla had more than **200 patents** and **patent applications**.

Into the Future

No one knows for sure how the automobile industry will evolve in the coming years. Certainly, more automakers are taking electric vehicles seriously. Most of the major automotive companies are working towards developing their own electric models. The question is if or when electric cars will overtake gas-powered vehicles in sales. Tesla remains committed to the idea of sustainable transportation and is constantly working to improve its technology. As a result, the company is likely to remain at the forefront of the electric automobile industry for a very long time.

Elon Musk has spoken of many ambitious plans for the company's future. At some point in 2018, Tesla plans to start manufacturing 10,000 vehicles each week. This increased production will be necessary to keep up with the many orders Tesla is receiving for the Model 3. Still, many people worry that this goal might be unrealistic. Regardless of what other people think, the CEO is likely to keep setting the bar high. To demonstrate this, he has also announced plans to build up to four more gigafactories in the near future.

In 2016, Tesla purchased SolarCity, a company that makes and installs solar panels. This purchase is in line with Tesla's goal of reducing dependence on fossil fuels through the creation of clean energy products. In the coming years, Tesla will continue to seek new opportunities toward this goal. If the purchase of SolarCity is any indication, Tesla will diversify into even more areas, making products that are affordable, sustainable, and efficient.

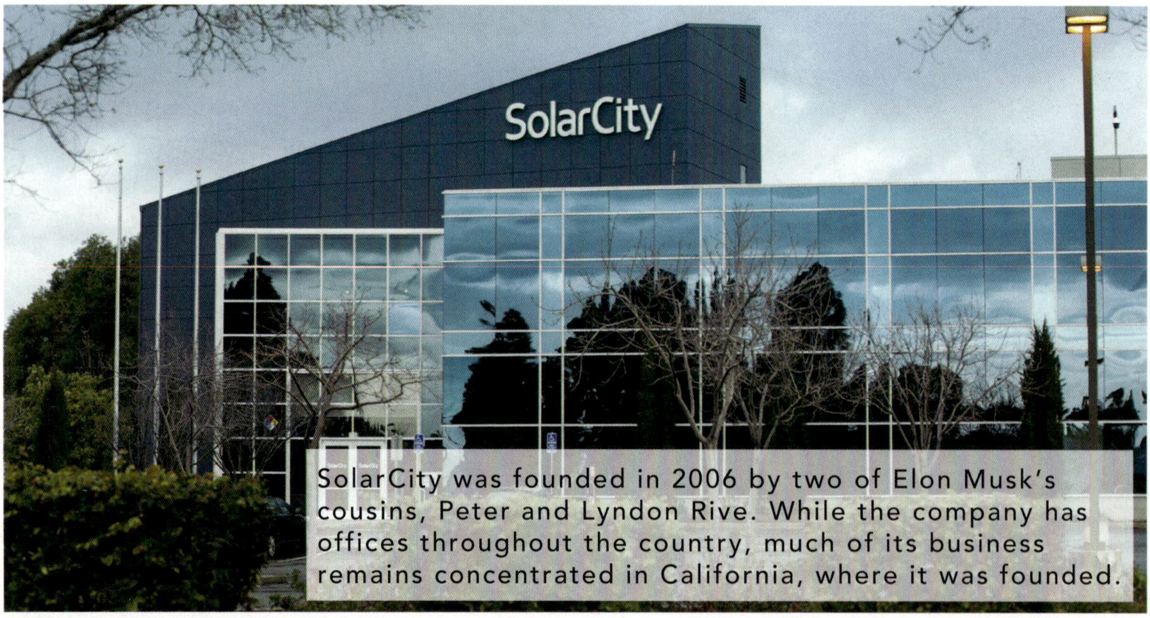

SolarCity was founded in 2006 by two of Elon Musk's cousins, Peter and Lyndon Rive. While the company has offices throughout the country, much of its business remains concentrated in California, where it was founded.

In 2017, Elon Musk unveiled the Tesla Semi, Tesla Motors' new electric semi truck. The truck has a 500-mile (805-km) range on one charge, even when it is fully loaded at a gross vehicle weight of 80,000 pounds (36,287 kg). Production of the truck is expected to begin in 2019.

Careers at Tesla

It takes a variety of workers to keep Tesla operating smoothly. Engineers often receive the most attention because they are the people who put the technology together. However, employees are also needed to design, build, and sell the company's battery-powered automobiles.

CEO

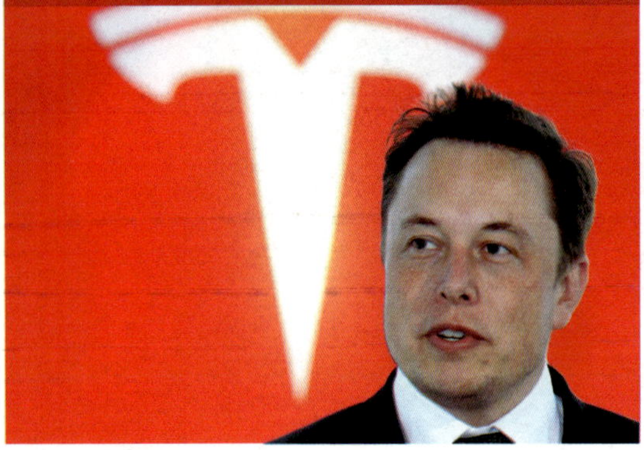

$38,000+ per year

The CEO is the highest-ranking person in a company. He or she is responsible for the operation of all the company's divisions. CEOs ensure that all divisions are running smoothly and are keeping their work within budget. The CEO is also responsible for the company's long-term planning. Working alongside other executives and senior management, he or she determines the direction the company will take over the next few years and implements an action plan to achieve these goals.

Product Specialist

$32,000–$40,000 per year

Tesla's product specialists work in the company's showrooms, where they greet customers and answer questions about Tesla vehicles. Product specialists also arrange test drives for customers who are interested in purchasing a Tesla. Product specialists work as **brand ambassadors** for the company. They must be knowledgeable about the company's products and be able to generate excitement when talking about them. An outgoing personality is a must.

Mechanical Engineer

$58,000–$136,000 per year

Tesla's mechanical engineers are responsible for designing the working parts of the company's vehicles. They may, for example, be involved in the design of the motor or the car's self-driving features. Since each part of the vehicle must work in cooperation with many other parts, mechanical engineers must be able to integrate their work into the car's overall design.

Assembly Technician

$42,000–$46,000 per year

Assembly technicians are the people who put Tesla's vehicles together. These workers use tools, machines, and their hands to build the many parts that make up an automobile. Each assembly technician is typically responsible for assembling one specific part of the vehicle. While they do not need an advanced degree, assembly technicians must have the training needed to perform this precise work.

Activity

Designing electric cars is one of the most challenging jobs at Tesla. These automobiles must be powerful, energy efficient, and safe. To attract buyers, they must also be pleasing to the eye.

Imagine that you are in charge of designing Tesla's next model. Make a list of the features your electric car design would include. Use the questions below to develop your concept. When you are done, create a drawing of what it would look like.

1. Who do you want to buy your car? Who will be riding in it?
2. What type of design will attract this type of buyer?
3. How will your car differ from other Tesla vehicles?
4. What will be your car's most distinguishing feature?
5. Which safety features will you put in your car?

Quiz

1 Where did the name of the company come from?

2 Who founded Tesla?

3 What was Tesla's first model of car called?

4 Who is the CEO of Tesla?

5 Where is Tesla's corporate headquarters?

6 What is Tesla's logo meant to resemble?

7 Who are three of Tesla's main competitors?

8 Which Tesla model is currently the fastest car in production?

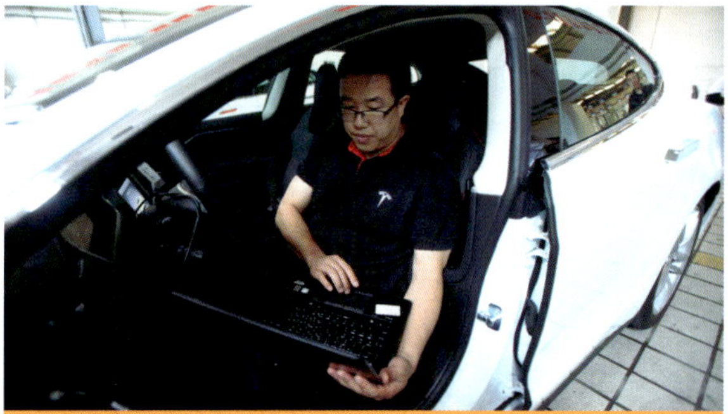

9 How many patents and applications did Tesla have when they were released to the public?

10 What did Tesla purchase in 2016?

Answers

1. Scientist Nikola Tesla **2.** Martin Eberhard and Marc Tarpenning **3.** Tesla Roadster **4.** Elon Musk **5.** Palo Alto, California **6.** The cross-section of an electric motor **7.** General Motors, Nissan, and BMW **8.** Model S **9.** More than 200 **10.** SolarCity

Key Words

alternating current: an electric current that reverses its direction many times per second at regular intervals

assets: valuable properties owned by a company or person

brand: a company's identity and image

brand ambassadors: people who are paid to promote a company's products

capital: money available for starting a business or investing

chairman of the board: the person who leads the board of directors, a group of people who oversee the direction a company is taking

clean energy: energy that does not pollute the environment when used

disposable: having a short time frame for use before wearing out

diversifying: enlarging or varying a company's range of products

entrepreneurs: people who organize and run their own business

environmentally friendly: not harmful to the environment

fossil fuels: natural fuels formed from the remains of living organisms

gigafactory: a large manufacturing plant

high-end: the most expensive range of products

hybrid: consisting of two different types, such as gasoline and electric power

internships: temporary jobs emphasizing on-the-job training

invested: committed money to a project in order to gain a financial return

liabilities: a company's debts and business costs

lithium-ion batteries: rechargeable batteries with twice the energy of standard batteries

logo: a symbol or design used to identify a specific company

market capitalization: the market value of a company's outstanding shares

philanthropy: making life better for other people

profits: money left over after expenses have been met

slogans: distinctive phrases used to identify specific companies or products

sustainable: capable of replenishing itself

Index

Published by Smartbook Media Inc.
350 5th Avenue, 59th Floor New York, NY 10118
Website: www.openlightbox.com

Editor: Heather Kissock
Designer: Nick Newton

Library of Congress Cataloging-in-Publication Data
Names: Gagne, Tammy, author.
Title: Tesla / Tammy Gagne.
Description: New York, NY : Smartbook Media Inc., [2019] | Series: Corporate America | Includes index.
Identifiers: LCCN 2017048292 (print) | LCCN 2017054301 (ebook) | ISBN 9781510534919 (Multi-User Ebook) | ISBN 9781510534902 (hard cover : alk.paper)
Subjects: LCSH: Tesla Motors--Juvenile literature. | Automobile industry and trade--United States--Juvenile literature. | Electric automobiles--United States--Juvenile literature. | Tesla automobiles--Juvenile literature.
Classification: LCC HD9710.U54 (ebook) | LCC HD9710.U54 T4743 2019 (print) |DDC 338.7/62922930973--dc23
LC record available at https://lccn.loc.gov/2017048292

Printed in Brainerd, Minnesota, United States
1 2 3 4 5 6 7 8 9 0 21 20 19 18 17

122017
151217

Photo Credits
Every reasonable effort has been made to trace ownership and to obtain permission to reprint copyright material. The publisher would be pleased to have any errors or omissions brought to its attention so that they may be corrected in subsequent printings. The publisher acknowledges Alamy, Getty Images, iStock, Newscom, and Shutterstock as its primary image suppliers for this title.